Terry

1.45

G000254720

DIESELS
in
SOUTH WALES

Michael Rhodes

Frontispiece: Canton Shed by night in 1964.

K. T. Symons

Oxford Publishing Company

Copyright © 1984 Oxford Publishing Co.

ISBN-0-86093-295-8

All rights reserved. No part of this book may be reproduced or transmitted in any form or by any means, electronic or mechanical, including photocopying, recording or any information storage and retrieval system, without permission in writing from the Publisher.

Typesetting by:
Aquarius Typesetting Services, New Milton, Hants.

Printed in Great Britain by:
Biddles Ltd., Guildford, Surrey.

Published by:
Oxford Publishing Co.
Link House
West Street
POOLE, Dorset

On 21st August 1964, ex-works Class 47 No. D1612 arrives at Pengam Yard with a freight train from the London Midland Region.

R. O. Tuck

A 'down' Pullman passing the new Canton Diesel Depot.

K. T. Symons

Introduction

South Wales has a dense network of railway lines, many of which are only used by freight trains, and of the 540 route miles in South Wales, half are for freight only. These lines serve over 35 collieries as well as numerous oil and chemical refineries, docks, cement works, quarries and power-stations. In comparison, the passenger service is quite simple, based on the main line from Fishguard to Severn Tunnel Junction and its branches.

Ever since travelling from Cardiff to Swansea in 1972 as a twelve year old trainspotter, I have been fascinated by the branch lines in South Wales. It was most confusing to see junction after junction on my way west when the official British Railways network map had no lines marked. In 1976 and 1977, I regularly cycled after school from my home to Radyr, and it was here that I spent many hours watching the coal trains as they descended from the Taff and Rhondda valleys. Another of my haunts was Pengam, which lacked the charm of Radyr with its semaphore signalling, but provided a greater variety of trains and motive power.

In September 1977 I bought an old Honda C70 from a close friend. Before crashing it one year later I managed to visit several of the Cardiff valleys as well as Graig Merthyr and Brynlliw. My interest in the railways of South Wales has remained undiminished by five years away at university and clinical school, although each holiday during this period has afforded me the opportunity to visit one or two more branch lines. The collection of photographs in this book is a complete record of my travels over the last seven years.

I am very grateful to Paul Shannon and Wyn Hobson for their photographs, which I have added to my collection, while Mr K. T. Symons and Mr R. O. Tuck were kind enough to provide me with several photographs taken in the early 1960s. I must also thank my parents for their continuing support, and Jenny for her patience.

Michael Rhodes
Oxford
May 1984

No. D7091 at Tyndall Field goods yard by night.   *K. T. Symons*

Chapter One
MAIN LINE ~ Severn Tunnel Junction to Gaer Junction and Abergavenny to Maindee Junction

The main line from Severn Tunnel Junction to Newport is one of the busiest and most interesting stretches in the country, with a tremendous variety of motive power traversing the line every day.

Severn Tunnel Junction Yard is the gateway to South Wales for all 'wagon load' traffic, and an important remarshalling point for Speedlink services. The yard has contracted far less than many other similar marshalling yards, and the only tracks not in use are the 'down' arrival sidings. The 'down' yard is still used, albeit as a flat yard which is shunted from the west end. On the 'up' side the old reception sidings, sometimes called Undy Yard, are used for Speedlink traffic whilst the 'up' yard is flat shunted from the east end. Up to 2,000 wagons are sorted each day at the yard, and these may be dispatched to the following destinations, most of which are served daily, some with as many as six trains:

Acton (2), Aintree, Ashton Gate, Barry, Bedwas, Bescot, Bridgend (2), Bristol, Cranmore, Dock Street, Dover, Eastleigh (2), East Usk (4), Ebbw Vale (2), Ellesmere Port, Exeter, Glascoed (2), Gloucester (2), Hallen Marsh, Haverton Hill, Kingsland Road, Llantrisant, Lydney, Machen (4), Margam (6), Moreton on Lugg, Mossend (3), Oakdale, Plymouth (3), Radyr (2), Reading, Ripple Lane, Scunthorpe (2), Swansea (3), Swindon, St. Blazey, Tidal (3), Tidenham (2), Tinsley,

Toton, Uskmouth, Warrington and Whitemoor.

As can be seen from the list, Severn Tunnel is very much the focal point for Railfreight in South Wales.

The British Steel Corporation (BSC) have two remaining steelworks in South Wales, both of which generate considerable traffic for British Rail. Llanwern is situated south of the main line, between Severn Tunnel Junction and Newport, this plant being officially opened by the Queen in 1962 and production commencing later the same year. Raw materials delivered to the works consist mainly of iron-ore from Port Talbot Docks, on the well-publicized 'Heaviest Train in Britain', and coal from the South Wales collieries with occasional extra train-loads from Staffordshire. Despatches of steel 'coils' and 'cut lengths' are forwarded to BSC Ebbw Vale and BSC Shotton and they are also exported via Newport, Swansea and Hamworthy Docks.

It seems unnecessary to describe the passenger service in detail, as information about this can easily be obtained from the public timetable. One further installation which deserves mention, however, is the Uskmouth Power-Station, which receives trains of oil from Herbrandston Refinery and coal from Marine and Bedwas collieries. It was opened in 1962, with up to six trainloads of coal each day travelling down to the power-station, and together with Llanwern Steelworks it uses most of the Eastern valleys coal.

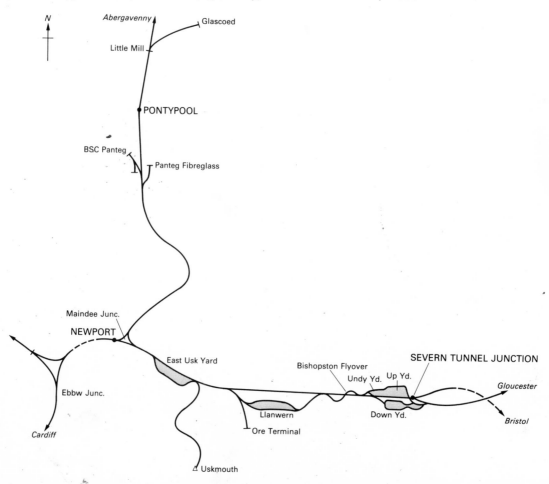

Plate 1: On 2nd October 1980, Class 25 No. 25296 stands waiting to enter the 'down' yard at Severn Tunnel Junction with the 7C62 15.43 service from Bristol (Kingsland Road). The VDA and VVVs contain traffic from Rowntrees at Avonmouth, whilst the CPVs are from the Avonside Wharf Blue Circle Cement terminal. All mixed freight traffic from Bristol and the South-West is now remarshalled at Severn Tunnel, and sent forward on one of the many services to the north and east.

Plate 2: Severn Tunnel Junction is served by trains from Cardiff to Bristol and also the less well-known service, hidden in table 56, from Cardiff to Gloucester. Providing a service to Caldicot, Chepstow and Lydney, there are six trains each way on weekdays. Here, a three car Swindon cross-country unit, No. C555, pauses at Severn Tunnel Junction with the 16.11 Newport to Worcester working. Many of the passengers are railmen based at Severn Tunnel, or railway enthusiasts visiting the nearby depot.

Plate 3:   A busy scene at Severn Tunnel Junction. A Swansea to Paddington express takes the London line over the 70m.p.h. turnout at Severn Tunnel, whilst Class 45 No. 45037 edges forward with the 7083, 03.20 Carlisle to Eastleigh freight service. As well as MOD traffic in VEVs and steel rail from Workington, the train contains a rake of new stone hoppers for utilization in the expanding stone traffic centred around Westbury.

Plate 4:   The reception sidings of Severn Tunnel Junction 'up' Yard have recently been converted into a Speedlink Yard, the 'up' yard being flat shunted from the Bristol end. Here Class 20 locomotives, Nos. 20017 and 20092, run round the 6V27, 06.32 working from Toton (West) Yard which, on 2nd October 1980, used the Undy Yard after closure of the 'down' yard hump. The engines will refuel at the depot and return north with the 8M43 train to Toton (New Bank).

Plate 5 (above): A special freight train made up of assorted mineral wagons (HTV, MDV, MCV) leaves the 'up' yard at Severn Tunnel behind Class 46 No. 46018. The train is bound for the sidings at Bristol (Parkway), from where the locomotive will proceed to Bristol (Kingsland Road) to pick up the 7C62 service to Severn Tunnel Junction.

Plate 6 (right): On a dismal day at the end of January 1983, Class 47 No. 47142 sneaks off one hour early with the 6M72, 14.05 Severn Tunnel to Warrington (Walton Old) Junction service. Amongst its assorted load is an ex-GWR gunpowder van (CXV), seen next to the engine.

Plate 7 (below): This train of covhops (CBA) from Tunstead to Margam (6V23) would normally pass Severn Tunnel at 01.00 hours. However, due to a locomotive failure in the Birmingham area the previous night, the train was stabled at Washwood Heath overnight. It is seen here, on 22nd January 1982, behind Class 47 No. 47480, running as the 6Z49 Washwood Heath to Margam Abbey. In the background Class 47 No. 47256 pokes its nose out of the cutting with the 6C39 from St. Blazey.

Plate 8 (left): Two air-braked freight trains stand side by side in Undy sidings at Severn Tunnel. On the left, Class 47 No. 47088 stands at the head of the 8V37, 03.27 service from Temple Mills, made up mostly of vans (VDA and VTG ferry vans). On the right Class 46 No. 46045 has just been uncoupled from the 6V47, 06.32 working from Toton.

Plate 10 (right upper): On 8th April 1982 the 6E64 service from Llandeilo Junction rounds the sharp curve at Undy, with ▶ Llanwern Steelworks in the background. Behind Class 47 No. 47122 there were, as well as standard Speedlink stock (VDA, BDA and OAA), some rather interesting SNCF flat wagons. Although the service is advertised as going to Haverton Hill, it is unlikely that any of the traffic seen here will reach the final destination. After shunting at Margam, Severn Tunnel Junction, Tinsley, Dringhouses and Tees, the train will eventually arrive at Haverton Hill the next morning.

Plate 11 (right middle): The 08.30 Manchester to Cardiff working had unusual motive power, on 23rd January 1982, in the form ▶ of Class 37 No. 37027. Just disappearing into the shadow of the Class 37 is Class 31 No. 31200, rushing by with an 'up' parcels train. It is interesting to compare Undy Yard on the left with *Plate 4*, taken just over a year earlier before the yard assumed its new role as Speedlink sidings.

Plate 12 (right lower): Having run west two hours earlier, Class 25 No. 25198 provides unusual motive power for the 4S88, 15.45 ▶ Pengam to Edinburgh Freightliner service, seen here at Bishopston.

Plate 9 (below): The Bishopston Flyover was built to allow access from the 'up' slow line, between Newport and Severn Tunnel Junction, to the 'up' yard at Severn Tunnel. The 9A75 train from Dock Street to Severn Tunnel Junction winds its way off the flyover behind Class 37 No. 37288.

Plate 13: One of the many destinations of coal from the eastern valleys is Uskmouth Power-Station, this being one of that dying breed still served by non-merry-go-round coal trains. The 6A84 train from Marine Colliery returns after unloading its coal at Uskmouth, and is seen here, on 23rd September 1982, at East Usk Junction behind Class 37 No. 37138.

Plate 14: With Llanwern Steelworks in the background, Class 37 No. 37294 eases the 9A75, 15.35 service to East Usk out of the vast complex. Traffic to the works includes iron-ore from Port Talbot Docks, coal from the eastern valleys and Llanharan, and oil from Llandarcy. Steel is dispatched to Ebbw Vale and Shotton for plating, and to Severn Tunnel Junction for distribution all over the country.

Plate 15: A very unusual visitor to South Wales was caught as it 'whistled' past East Usk on 30th March 1983. The 6V90 Carlisle (Kingmoor) to Severn Tunnel Junction train was hauled by Class 40 No. 40069, and was made up of one STV, three VVVs and a 45 ton tank, all of which are available in model form. Although short trains are loss sustaining for BR, they are certainly useful for the railway modeller.

Plate 16: As well as multiple units, locomotives from classes 25, 31, 33, 35, 45, 46 and 47 have all hauled trains from Bristol to Cardiff over the last ten years. The service is now dealt with by Class 33s, with the occasional Class 31 being slipped in for variety. Here, on 23rd September 1982, Class 31 No. 31286 rounds the curve at East Usk Junction with the 15.45 Bristol (Temple Meads) to Cardiff service.

Plate 17 (left upper): The low evening sun highlights the houses along the line at East Usk, while eight empty BBAs rattle along behind Class 37 No. 37291, and form the 4F03 Ebbw Vale to Llanwern service. In the background, a rake of 'sea lion' hoppers heads west behind Class 37 No. 37185, the train being the 6A70, 15.20 Severn Tunnel Junction to Machen Quarry.

Plate 18 (left lower): In industrial guise, ex-BR Class 03, No. 2181, is called *Pride of Gwent*. The locomotive is used to shunt the Gwent coal depot which lies in the centre of Newport, and is reached by the branch from Waterloo Loop Junction. In the background is the transporter bridge across the Usk, one of only two in Britain, the other being in Middlesbrough.

Plate 19: It was in May 1977 that the full HST service from Paddington to Bristol and South Wales was introduced. This transformed what was one of British Rail's slower Inter-City services into the second fastest regular Inter-City service in the world. An example of the exceptional running on this line is provided by the 15.15 Paddington to Swansea service which, on 30th January 1981, left Paddington on time and was passing mile post 110½ just one hour later! Not travelling at quite that speed, unit No. 253031 leaves Newport with the 15.40 Paddington to Cardiff train on 23rd September 1983.

Plate 20: In the 1960s, trains from Cardiff to the North-West ran via Shrewsbury, giving the route Inter-City status. During the early and mid-1970s the service was reduced to an all stations diesel multiple unit working. This was then upgraded to locomotive and coaches in 1977, with the Class 25s providing the motive power. In order to cut journey times the haulage was changed to the more powerful Class 33 locomotives in May 1981. With Newport Town Hall in the background, Class 33 No. 33014 leaves Newport with the 15.10 Cardiff to Crewe service.

Plate 22 (left): Freight trains are a rare sight on Saturdays although there are, however, a few Speedlink services timetabled to run over the weekend. One of these is the 6V39, 05.44 ABS from Mossend to Severn Tunnel Junction. Class 47 No. 47087, followed by five BBAs carrying steel coil, one OBA and a ferry van, passes Pontypool on Saturday, 7th August 1982.

Plate 21 (left top): The BSC Panteg Works, between Pontypool and Newport, maintains its rail link but neither dispatches nor receives any traffic by rail at the moment. Similarly, the spur in the foreground runs to modern loading facilities at Panteg Fibre-glass which, by the quality of the rust on the tracks, obviously makes very little use of its rail link. The 16.02 Crewe to Cardiff train, hauled by Class 33 No. 33008, is seen passing Panteg and running ten minutes late.

Plate 24 (above): Class 47 No. 47230 approaches Pontrilas with the 6S98, 07.55 Severn Tunnel Junction to Mossend service. Included in the train formation are MDV coal wagons, VVV vans, fuel oil tanks for BR diesel depots and a few antiquated steel coil wagons, some dating back to GWR days.

Paul D. Shannon

Plate 23 (left lower): This rather nice view is of the 08.01 Crewe to Cardiff train passing through Pontrilas on 13th April 1982, with Eastleigh-based Class 33 No. 33031 in charge.

Paul D. Shannon

Plate 25 (above): Having got rather dirty since its naming earlier in the year, Class 33 No. 33027 *Earl Mountbatten of Burma* accelerates out of Pontypool Road with the 12.25 Crewe to Cardiff working.

Plate 26 (below): Although steel production ceased at Shotton in 1979, steel is still tin plated there. For eighteen months after the closure, special services ran from Shotton to Llanwern to clear the iron-ore stock piled in the North Wales plant. Now trains of coil run from Llanwern to Shotton, and an example of this service is provided by the 6Z81, 18.00 Llanwern to Dee Marsh train, seen here, behind Class 37 No. 37294, passing Pontypool.

Plate 28 (right): Three trains run from the Glasgow area to Severn Tunnel Junction each day, with two being from Mossend Yard and the other being the 6V39, 08.07 Ravenscraig No. 3 to Severn Tunnel Junction. This service is seen here at Panteg, with a rake of 45 ton oil tanks (TTB) being followed by two VDAs with Class 47 No. 47237 as the motive power.

Plate 27 (above): This really is an ideal prototype for the railway modeller where Class 25 No. 25248 is followed by three VVVs and two HTVs. From its size, one might think this was a local trip freight, however it is the 6V90, 05.57 Carlisle to Severn Tunnel Junction working, seen here crossing the River Usk just north of Newport. Since October 1982 this train has been TWThO, probably due to the light loading during the summer of 1982. Although there are two trains from Carlisle to Severn Tunnel Junction, there are no return workings. Traffic for the north travels on one of the three services to Mossend, or the 14.05 to Warrington.

Chapter Two

For some twenty years there has been no passenger service in the Eastern Valleys, although an extensive rail network remains to cater for the collieries and other industry in the area. Until the closure of the steelworks at Ebbw Vale in 1978 the main line from Newport was double track throughout and very heavily used. During 1981/2 the line was singled from Park Junction to Lime Kiln Junction, and from Aberbeeg to Waunllwyd at Ebbw Vale.

The British Steel Corporation (BSC) have a tin plate works at Ebbw Vale, and this receives 12,000 tons of hot rolled coil each week. Some 6,000 tons of this comes from BSC Llanwern, just 22 miles away, 2,000 tons from BSC Margam and 4,000 tons from BSC Ravenscraig in Scotland. The rail output from the works is 3,000 tons of tin plate, two-thirds of which goes to various destinations in the UK, the rest being exported via Newport Docks.

Of the collieries in the area, Oakdale is by far the largest, being opened in 1910 and producing an output of 14,000 tons of coal each week. A major reorganization project, completed in 1980, linked neighbouring Markham and Celynen North collieries to Oakdale by underground roadways, this creating one railhead for the seven faces being worked in the three collieries. Future plans for extension will open up more reserves to the south of Oakdale, making it the largest colliery in South Wales, with a target output of 900,000 tons annually. Five trains each day take coal from the colliery to East Usk Yard and Severn Tunnel Junction Yard, from where it is sent to Port Talbot, Nantgarw or Dawes Lane in Scunthorpe. Some trains travel directly to BSC Llanwern.

One of the smaller collieries in the area is Celynen South, which opened in 1890. Its weekly output of 2,300 tons is sent to BSC Llanwern.

Private enterprise is the hallmark of the Machen branch, which terminates at the Bedwas coke ovens owned by British Benzol & Coal Distillation Ltd. It is here that coking coal from Cwm, Tymawr, Trelewis and Marine collieries is converted into foundry coke, which is distributed all over Britain. Further down the branch towards Newport are the Powell Duffryn quarries at Machen, which supply British Rail with 6,000 tons of rail ballast each week. This is shunted in the company's sidings by two Plant 0-4-0 diesels, and then pushed out of the plant to be collected by BR four times each day.

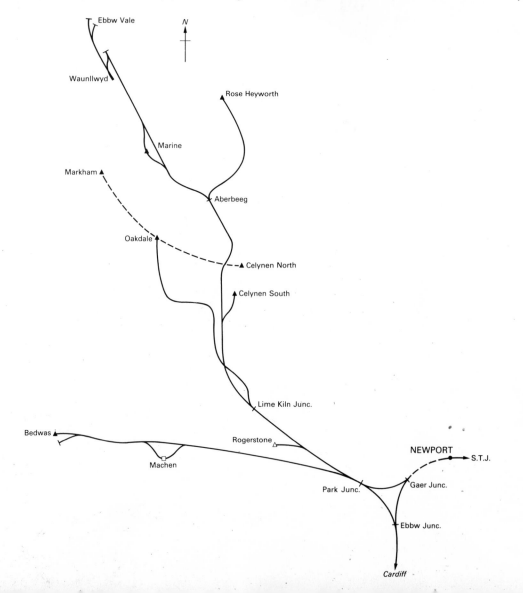

Plate 29: Park Junction had a complex layout before its rationalization during 1981, although much of the redundant trackwork had not yet been removed when this photograph was taken on 23rd June 1982. The line on the left climbs from Gaer Junction *(see Plate 32)*, the central line used to go down to the yards at Alexander Dock Junction and the line on the right descends to Ebbw Junction. Empty 21 ton mineral wagons (MDV) from East Usk to Trethomas Colliery are seen being hauled by Class 37 No. 37227 on the 6A77 service.

Plate 30: The signal box at Park Junction was still open in June 1982, as Class 37 No. 37295 brings ballast from Machen Quarry down to the main line. The train is the 6A70 working to Severn Tunnel Junction, from where the ballast will be dispatched to South Wales and further afield on the network.

Plate 31: A special consignment of steel, bound for the BSC tin plate works at Ebbw Vale, is taken up the valley by Class 37 No. 37273. The train, seen here at Park Junction, is made up of VDAs, KTAs, SPAs and BBAs, and is running as the 6Z02 service from Severn Tunnel Junction.

Plate 32: The empty trackbed on the branch from Gaer Junction to Park Junction is evidence of the recent singling of this line. Class 37 No. 37175 approaches Park Junction with the 6A83 tea-time working to Oakdale Colliery.

Plate 33: Lime Kiln Junction is the next box up the valley after Park Junction and this photograph, taken in July, captures the rural atmosphere of the junction. There are old style crossing gates, gas lamps and an old stone cabin beyond the gates which date back nearly 100 years. Class 37 No. 37158 rumbles up the valley 'engine and van' to pick up a load of coal from Marine Colliery.

Plate 34: The line from Park Junction to Lime Kiln Junction was singled during 1981 as part of the rationalization of the Eastern Valleys and it was also realigned at Rogerstone due to road building north of Newport. The 6A93 Waunllwyd to Severn Tunnel Junction service is made up of empty BBAs, on 23rd June 1983, with Class 37 No. 37254 in charge. Rogerstone Power-Station, in the background, is served by road, but during the realignment of the main line, the sidings to the power-station were kept intact, as can be seen from the photograph.

Plate 35 (left upper): Shortly before joining the main Ebbw Vale route at Lime Kiln Junction, Class 37 No. 37255 passes through the village of Penar with an Oakdale to Radyr coal train on 13th April 1983.

Paul D. Shannon

Plate 36 (left lower): Class 37 No. 37229 brings coal down from Markham Colliery and passes a merry-go-round train for Aberthaw loading at Oakdale Colliery. Two weeks after this photograph was taken, in July 1979, the branch to Markham Colliery closed with the coal being brought to the surface at Oakdale.

Plate 37 (above): A couple of sheep are grazing on the platform at Llanhillieth which has not seen a passenger train since 1962. Under the shadow of some rather unusual terraced houses, Class 37 No. 37285 brings its thirty loaded MDVs slowly down the valley. This coal, like most from the Eastern Valleys, is bound for Uskmouth Power-Station, this particular train being the 6A82 Marine Colliery to Uskmouth working.

Plate 38 (below): On 23rd June 1982, the 4F03 Ebbw Vale to Llanwern service is seen running three hours late, not an unusual occurrence, as coil trains are one of the worst timekeepers in South Wales. On the left, one of the NCBs industrial locomotives shunts at the northern entrance to Marine Colliery and the author's car can be seen perched on the pavement, out of the way of passing lorries and buses on the A4046.

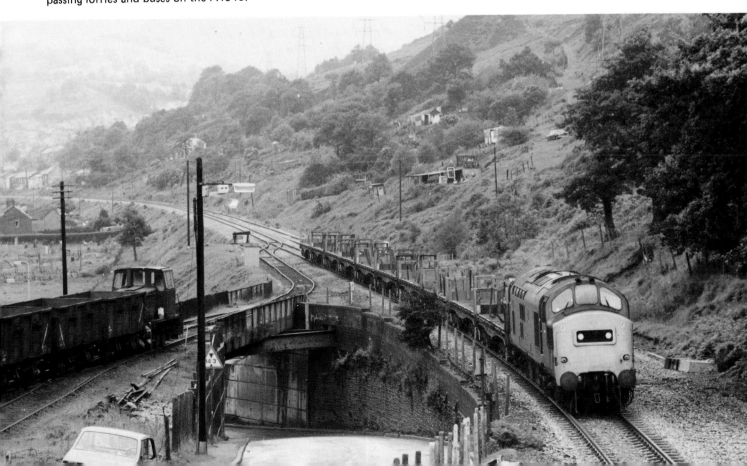

Plate 39: The rain streams down on Class 37 No. 37304 at Trethomas Station, which was originally on the Brecon & Merthyr Railway. To reach Merthyr, trains had to run on Rhymney lines from Bargoed to Deri Junction. The locomotive arrived from Severn Tunnel Junction and will leave with its load of coal as the 6A70 to Radyr. Not only Bedwas Colliery can be seen in the background, but also the British Benzole Coke Works.

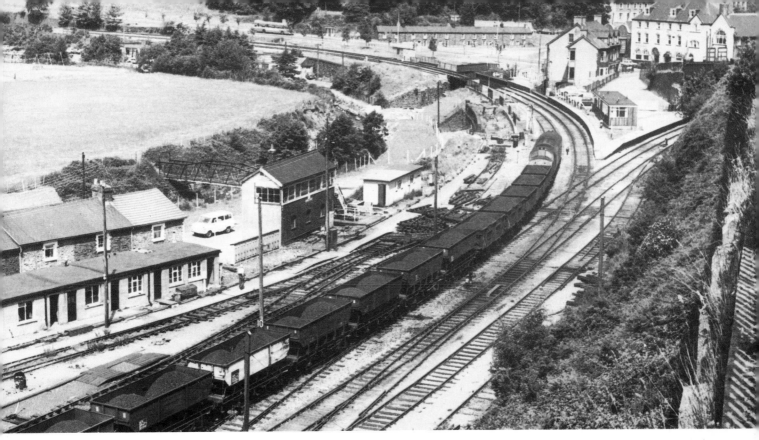

Plate 40: During July 1979 an unidentified Class 37 hauls a mixture of MDV, HTV and HTO wagons with coal for Ebbw Vale.

Plate 41: The single track branch from Aberbeeg to Rose Heyworth Colliery is operated on the 'one train working' principle. Thus, on the morning of 13th April 1982 Class 37 No. 37241 waits for its train of 36 MDVs to be loaded by mechanical shovel, before proceeding as the 6A85 working to Margam Yard.

Paul D. Shannon

Chapter Three
MAIN LINE ~ Gaer Junction to Water Street Junction

The South Wales main line is four-tracked from Gaer Junction to just west of Cardiff, from where it continues as double track to Newlands Junction. Cardiff is the capital city of Wales and, with a population of 270,000, it naturally has the largest passenger station in South Wales. Not only does Cardiff (Central) serve the city itself but, by connections from the five branches which radiate from the city, another 500,000 people are able to use the station as their link with the Inter-City network. The 88 main line departures each weekday are divided, according to their final destinations, as follows:

London (26), Swansea (21), Bristol (7), Crewe (6), Portsmouth (5), Birmingham and Milford Haven (3), Weymouth, Gloucester, Newcastle, Newport and Fishguard Harbour (all 2) and, finally, one each to Swindon, Chepstow, Worcester, Manchester, Leeds, Hereford and Carmarthen.

In addition to these there are over 100 departures each day on the five main branches from the capital. The 'panel' at Cardiff handles in excess of 350 train movements over 24 hours so that as well as 200 passenger departures, there are 150 other movements. These are made up of light engine workings, empty stock trains and, most importantly, freight services.

Having lived in Cardiff since 1962, I have been fortunate enough to photograph most types of main line locomotive passing through Central Station. In fact, the only classes never seen at Cardiff are the Scottish Region's Class 26 and 27 locomotives. The large motive power depot at Canton has an allocation of 39 shunting locomotives and 123 main line diesels, and with over forty locomotives being shedded there at weekends, there is plenty of interest for visiting trainspotters!

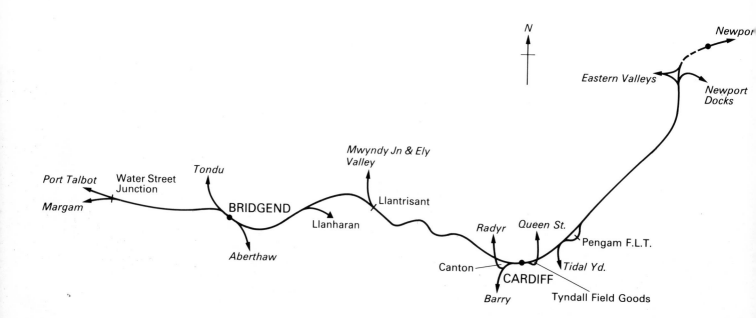

Plate 42a: One week prior to the installation of multiple aspect signalling, Class 52 'Western' No. D1039 passes the old Pengam box with an 'up' express. This scene, photographed on 28th May 1966, provides a remarkable contrast to a similar view which can be seen in *Plate 45*.

R. O. Tuck

Plate 42b: On 30th May 1968, Class D95XX diesel-hydraulic No. D9528 passes Pengam Yard with a short trip freight working to Tidal Sidings. As can be seen, the old flat yard has been completely demolished and replaced by a Freightliner terminal.

R. O. Tuck

Plate 43:   The evening sun highlights the bonnet of Class 37 No. 37129 as it passes Gaer Junction, on 23rd September 1982, with the 11 x 100 ton oil tanks which are returning empty from Oakleigh sidings to Robeston sidings in West Wales. Rail traffic from the refineries has been decreasing since 1968 when a staggering 85 per cent of oil from coastal refineries to inland distribution centres went by rail. The announcement of the closure of Esso's Herbrandston Refinery, with the loss of 250 jobs, can only mean a further reduction in the amount of oil travelling by rail in South Wales.

Plate 44:   The 4S81 Pengam to Glasgow Freightliner is often double-headed by a Class 47 and a Class 37. Having driven from Oxford, after a Friday afternoon ward round, I was rather unlucky to find only Class 47 No. 47501 in charge as the train passed Ebbw Junction on 20th August 1982. Of the 25 vehicles on the train not all are bound for Glasgow as, in fact, only five are. Five go to Edinburgh and fifteen are detached at Crewe, from whence ten go to Trafford Park and the remaining five to Garston.

Plate 45: The 4E70 Danygraig to Stratford Freightliner stops for 45 minutes at Pengam to have the Cardiff portion of this train added. On 19th May 1977, Class 45 'Peak' No. 45002 arrives at Pengam with its load. On the left, the line to Tidal sidings can just be seen, and on the right Roath goods sidings are just visible.

Plate 46: Like an arrow, the 17.15 Paddington to Swansea train streaks across the Marshfield Flats on a sunny evening in April 1982. The train is passing Coedkernew, and across the channel the town of Clevedon is clearly visible.

Plate 47: Class 25 locomotives used to be a regular sight in South Wales on both freight and passenger workings. However, since the Western Region has lost its Class 25 allocation and the Cardiff to Crewe service has been taken over by Class 33s, they have become increasingly rare. In 1977, when they were still an everyday sight, Class 25 No. 25264 passes Pengam with the 8V99, 12.19 Crewe to Cardiff Tidal sidings or Radyr mineral train.

Plate 48: For the last five years the 7C43, 10.25 Severn Tunnel Junction to Llandeilo Junction service has appeared regularly in the working timetable. The train refuses to die, having been maintained in the October 1982 timetable, although Llandeilo Junction Yard has been closed. In more prosperous days Class 47 No. 47052 passes Pengam with the 7C43 train, comprised mostly of scrap metal bound for the now closed Duports Steelworks in Llanelli.

Plates 49 & 50: Two photographs taken on 26th February 1977, showing the last day of the diesel-hydraulic 'Westerns'. As well as D1013 and D1023 with the final 'Western' special *(right)*, enthusiasts were treated to the sight of two Class 40s on football specials for the fifth round FA cup tie between Cardiff and Everton. *(Above)* Class 40 No. 40120 winds its way slowly into Cardiff (Central) with its load of Everton supporters.

Plate 51: Summer Saturday traffic in South Wales is fairly heavy, with trains to Tenby and Pembroke Dock as well as extra services on lines such as Cardiff to Portsmouth. Here, the 12.25 Cardiff to Portsmouth train leaves the capital behind Class 47 No. 47488. To the left is the derelict Tyndall Field goods yard, and on the right the abandoned NCL depot, a sorry sight indeed.

Plates 52 (left) & 54 (right): On 29th January 1978, Cardiff saw its second 'Deltic' with an enthusiasts' special. Class 55 No. 55018 *Ballymoss* came off the train at Cardiff (Central) *(right)* and Class 20 locomotives Nos. 20030 and 20142 took the train on to Treherbert, providing a rare feast for Cardiff's trainspotters.

Plate 53: The 10.25 Bristol (Temple Meads) to Cardiff train passes Windsor Bridge on 21st September 1979. The train is hauled by Class 31 No. 31414, one of the Class 31/4 locomotives allocated to the Western Region. At the start of October 1982, the Western Region lost all its Class 31/4 allocation to March, the remaining diagrams behind handed over to the Class 47s.

Plate 55 (right): This is what happens when you allow your younger brother to go to the station without you! On 24th November 1979, a special from Bangor to Barry Island arrives at Cardiff (Central) behind Class 40 No. 40107. This photograph was taken by my youngest brother David, using a Zenith EM camera. The locomotive returned north later in the day with a Cardiff to Crewe train.

D. J. Rhodes

Plate 56 (below): Although Class 50 locomotives are allocated to Laira and Old Oak Common, and have been shedded at Bristol (Bath Road), they are extremely rare in South Wales. Deputizing for a failed Class 47, Class 50 No. 50027 winds into the carriage sidings at Canton at the head of a Paddington to Cardiff service.

Plate 57 (above): After the replacement of Class 52s by Class 47 locomotives on the South Wales to Paddington expresses, they were relegated to the Paddington to Fishguard boat-train and other trains from Cardiff to Bristol and Plymouth. In December 1976, Class 52 'Western' No. D1048 *Western Lady* passes Cardiff (Canton) with the Fishguard boat-train.

Plate 59 (right upper): Passing the site of Llantrisant Station is Class 37 No. 37302 with a train of coal from Llanharan Colliery to ▶ BSC Llanwern. In the background is Llantrisant Goods Depot and the line to Cwm and Coed Ely.

Plate 60 (right lower): Driver Ranson is about to climb into the cab of Class 37 No. 37239 as the shunter trudges to the weigh- ▶ bridge at Llanharan to ring the panel. As soon as the panel have room on the main line, the train will get under way to Llanwern.

Plate 58 (below): One from the archives, taken with an old Agfa Stillette, is the 6V10 Guide Bridge parcels train. This working regularly brought Class 40 and 'foreign' Class 25 locomotives to Cardiff and, on 11th October 1975, Class 24 No. 24087 arrives at Cardiff with its load of Christmas mail. The train ran from the beginning of the winter timetable to Christmas Eve each year, with 1975 being the last year for this train.

Plate 61: Although at first, this looks like a block oil train, the last wagon, an OBA containing concrete sleepers, gives it away as the 6C22, 07.00 Severn Tunnel Junction to Llandeilo Junction 'air brakes'. It is seen here behind Class 47 No. 47225 passing Brynna, near Bridgend, on 25th October 1982.

Plate 62: The 4V66, 01.45 Stratford to Danygraig Freightliner passes Brynna, on the morning of 25th October 1982, behind Class 47 No. 47251. The terminal at Danygraig was opened in 1969, and had several services offering through carriage of goods to Willesden, Sheffield, Harwich, Liverpool, Manchester and Birmingham, although the only train west of Pengam in 1982 was the Stratford service.

Chapter Four
Cardiff Docks and the Vale of Glamorgan

This chapter contains a contrast in types of railway operation, from the sprawling and inefficient Tidal sidings, past the 1960s-built Aberthaw Power-Station, to the Speedlink terminal of the 1980s at the Bridgend Ford Motor Co. plant.

Cardiff Docks was once the largest exporter of coal in the UK, and the Roath branch was constructed in order to allow direct access from the Merthyr and Treherbert valleys to the vast Tidal Yard. The branch was closed in the mid-1960s, but the large layout at Tidal still remains, with over sixty tracks still intact. Since the closure of East Moors Steelworks and the departure of much heavy industry from the dock area, this has become very under-used. There are three departures each day to Severn Tunnel Junction, two to Radyr and a newly-introduced Speedlink service, the 6E44, 08.50 to Scunthorpe (Trent) Yard. There are further departures to Uskmouth, Barry and twice a week to Old Oak Common, all fitted into a twelve hour shift starting at eight in the morning.

Allied Steel & Wire Ltd. now own the GKN Castle and Tremorfa Works, and are the main rail customers in the dock area. Tremorfa Steelworks has a production capacity of 500,000 tons of steel billet per year, this being processed at the Cardiff Rod Mill and the Tremorfa Bar Plant. As well as locally produced steel, additional steel billets are brough by rail from Scunthorpe, Sheffield and Poole Docks. The total output of Allied Steel is 15,000 tons of wire rod and 500 tons of steel bar each week, and this is sent by rail to the West Midlands, Sheffield, London, Glasgow, Gateshead and Warrington.

Barry Docks export coal, mainly from Abercwmboi and Nantgarw and also, rather curiously, grain from Newmarket.

Woodham Bros. steam scrap-yard made Barry into a household name for most railway enthusiasts but also of interest, however, is the nearby British Rail stabling point which acts as host to locomotives working to and from Aberthaw Power-Station, and which, on a Saturday night, may house up to twenty locomotives.

The previous descriptions of rail traffic pale into insignificance when compared with the amount of coal and the number of trains which run to keep the 'coal mountains' at Aberthaw stocked. There are fifteen trains every day to the power-station, all of which are hauled to Aberthaw Yard by two Class 37 locomotives. They are then taken into the power-station itself by one of the two Class 47s allocated to shuttle coal round the large rail loop at Aberthaw. The weekly tonnage supplied by different collieries does vary, but a typical week is as follows:

Blaenant 35,000 tons, Taff Merthyr 12,000 tons, Lady Windsor 12,000 tons, Penallta 10,000 tons, Ogmore Vale 5,000 tons and Cwm Bargoed 4,000 tons.

A recent development at the western end of the Vale of Glamorgan line is the construction of new sidings at the Ford Motor Co. plant in Bridgend. The plant was opened in 1980 and the two trains each day from Severn Tunnel Junction bring cylinder blocks and crankshafts from Dagenham, and cylinder heads from Italy to the works. The return trains take finished Escort engines bound for Halewood, Saarlouis in Germany and Valencia in Spain.

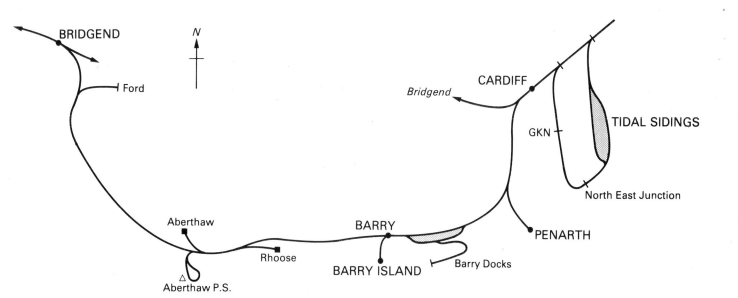

Plate 63:   Sleeping deep in the Cardiff dockland, Class 08 locomotives Nos. 08194 and 08352 have very little work to do on the afternoon of 20th May 1978. Traffic has decreased gently since the closure of the East Moors Steelworks, but some steel still travels by rail to and from the GKN Works in the area.

Plate 64:   Coal from America was imported via Newport and Cardiff docks for over a year, starting in 1979. However, the threat of industrial action by the miners of South Wales brought this to an end at the beginning of 1980. A large amount of coal was stockpiled, and trains continued to run from the docks to Didcot Power-Station for six months after the coal stopped arriving. On 26th May 1980, Class 56 No. 56045 arrives at Tidal sidings with empties from Didcot Power-Station.

Plate 65:   The extensive track layout at the south end of Cardiff Docks is controlled by the North-East Junction signal box. The signalman takes a rest curled up on the bench on the right, there being no more than six trains during his eight hour shift.

Plate 66:   An unusual visitor to Tidal sidings during May 1977 was Class 37 No. 37080. It leaves the yard with the 7M60, 19.50 Cardiff to Bescot working.

Plate 67: In pouring rain during September 1982, the 6090 Taff Merthyr to Aberthaw Power-Station working passes Barry Town Station, on which Class 37 locomotives Nos. 37205 and 37257 near the end of their thirty mile journey from the colliery. A pair of Class 37s pick up another merry-go-round train from the sidings in the background in an effort to satisfy the almost insatiable appetite of the power-station, and this will follow the 6090.

Plate 68: Empty grain wagons return from J. Rank Ltd., of Atlantic Mills in Barry Docks. The grain from Newmarket has come to Barry on the 6C00, 14.25 Plymouth (Friary) to Barry Docks service, which it joined at Severn Tunnel Junction. The wagons will return east on the 7B14 Barry (High Level) to Plymouth (Friary) working, then from Severn Tunnel to Whitemoor and on to Cambridge and finally Newmarket.

Plate 69: The 10.20 Rhymney to Barry Island train passes Barry Docks on 14th June 1982.

Plate 70: A busy scene at Aberthaw, with the 6C86 cement train to Radyr leaving behind Class 47 No. 47233. The other cement wagons left in the station will travel to Barry and then Severn Tunnel Junction on the 7B14 service, from where they will reach their destinations around the country. In the background, Class 47 No. 47230 draws forward with a merry-go-round for the power-station. As the length of the merry-go-round train has increased, so has the size of the pilots needed for the power-station, resulting in Class 47 locomotives being used. In 1980, a pair of Class 20s was borrowed from Haymarket to take trains into the power-station, although they returned north after only two weeks due to problems with slipping.

Plate 71 (below): Coal not only comes from the Cardiff valleys to Aberthaw, but also from further west, and Brynlliw and Blaengarw collieries have services to the power-station. Here the 6083 merry-go-round train from Jersey Marine storage sidings arrives at Aberthaw behind Class 37s Nos. 37288 and 37297. In the background is the Aberthaw Cement Works.

Chapter Five

With the closure of the branch from Aber Junction to Walnut Tree Junction, all trains from this area must travel through Cardiff (Central) in order to leave the valley. Several years ago this would have caused severe congestion at Cardiff (Queen Street) and on the through lines of platforms 6 and 7 at Cardiff (Central). The closure of Bargoed Colliery and the tar plant at Caerphilly, together with modernization of the four remaining collieries in this area, enabling them to accept merry-go-round wagons, has considerably reduced the number of trains on the line.

On the passenger side there are fourteen trains each day from Rhymney to Cardiff, continuing to Penarth or Barry. But unlike the other two valleys there are additional trains from points nearer Cardiff with two from Bargoed, four from Ystrad Mynach and four from Aber. Finally, within Cardiff itself, is the Coryton branch which leaves the main line at Heath Junction and has five stations along its 2¼ miles, four of them within 1¼ miles of each other. Not even the Southern Region can compete with this for frequency of stations, but with only twelve trains each way on weekdays, traffic is very light on this branch.

The three collieries at Penallta, Taff Merthyr and Deep Navigation each contribute over 10,000 tons of coal every week to the massive Aberthaw Power-Station. Penallta Colli-

ery, built between 1906 and 1909, is one of the deepest pits in South Wales and its weekly output of 10,500 tons is sent on nine trains to Aberthaw. The fourteen trains each week from Taff Merthyr Colliery carry in excess of 12,000 tons of coal, whereas nearby Deep Navigation Colliery has only six departures each week. Unlike the collieries already mentioned, the colliery at Cwmbargoed is not owned by the NCB, but by three private contractors. During 1983, A. J. Williams had a contract with the CEGB to provide three trainloads of coal each week. The line to Cwmbargoed continues further west, perched precariously on the hillside above Merthyr, to Dowlais Foundry, from where occasional loads of steel castings are dispatched on the 9C84 trip to Radyr Yard.

The state of the rail network in this area is fairly stable and the only foreseeable changes are the closure of the coal depot at Rhymney, and perhaps the eventual closure of the Coryton branch. Signal boxes at Heath, Aber, Ystrad Mynach and Bargoed control the whole valley, although the box at Heath Junction will be replaced by a 'panel' box within the next year, and it is inevitable that Aber box will collect a fair number of 'white' or disused levers with the closure of the branch to Taffs Well. This leaves a rather vestigial signal system for such a large area.

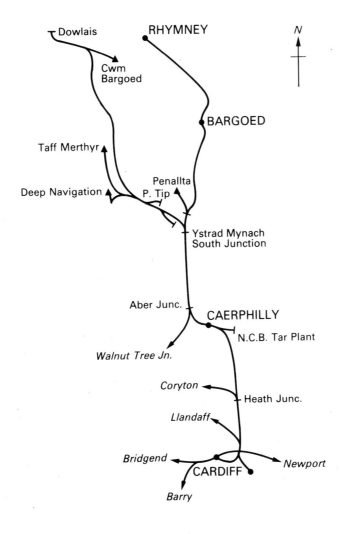

Plate 73 (above): Signalman Price keeps his log up to date as another of the hourly suburban services makes its way past Heath Junction on the long journey up the valley to Rhymney. The box at Heath is a fringe box to the panel at Cardiff, and as such has a train describer box to dial the reporting numbers of trains through to the panel. This piece of modern equipment contrasts strongly with the gas lamps, clearly seen in this picture.

Plate 74 (below): Plans exist to demolish the existing signal box at Heath Junction and build a small panel box 200 yards further north on the other side of the line. This development would also involve a housing estate on the site of the present junction, and a new junction a quarter of a mile further north. Passing the box during January 1979 is the daily trip from Caerphilly to Radyr, behind Class 37 No. 37281. This working has ceased since the closure of the NCB tar plant at Caerphilly.

Plate 72 (left): With the ill-fated Brunel House in the background, a three car Derby suburban unit, No. C304, approaches Heath Junction with a tea-time train from Penarth to Rhymney in April 1981.

Plate 75 (above): It is unusual to be able to photograph a train at one station from the next station along the line. However, this can be done on the Coryton branch. From the platform at Coryton, a Cardiff bound train is seen leaving Whitchurch Station on a very dull and rainy day in February 1983.

Plate 76 (below): Standing at Coryton, on 26th February 1983, a three car Derby suburban unit, No. C315, awaits departure as the 13.00 service to Cardiff (Bute Road). The existence of this branch is threatened almost annually, and it seems unlikely that it will survive into the 1990s.

Plate 77 (right upper): The points and signals are set for Class 37 locomotives, Nos. 37280 and 37298, to descend the 'big hill' from Aber Junction to Walnut Tree Junction with the 6094 Ocean to Aberthaw service. During 1982, this line was worked as a single line and then completely closed. What appears a rather inflated estimate of £250,000 was given as the cost of modifying track and signalling to operate the 'big hill' as a single track branch, and it does not look as if the line will ever open again.

Plate 78 (right lower): On a glorious day during June 1982, Class 37 locomotives, Nos. 37296 and 37287, wind their way out of the complex of buildings at Taff Merthyr Colliery. At 15.00 they will depart on their thirty mile journey as the 6092 service to Aberthaw.

Plate 79 (left): Poised precariously on a rock in the middle of the stream, I was fortunate to capture Class 37 locomotives Nos. 37296 and 37287 loading the 6092 working to Aberthaw at Taff Merthyr. My enthusiasm for this picture was somewhat 'dampened' by events that followed immediately after pressing the shutter!

Plate 80 (above): In February 1983, Penallta Colliery was supplying two trainloads of coal each day to Aberthaw Power-Station. A fairly constant feature in the very variable merry-go-round timetable is the 6090 Barry to Penallta and return working. The train is pictured here, on 30th June 1982, behind Class 37 locomotives, Nos. 37277 and 37288, at Ystrad Mynach Station.

Plate 81 (below): Spoil from the collieries at Taff Merthyr and Deep Navigation is transported to Nelson Bog for dumping at Penallta Junction Tip. This is done using 34 ton capacity HKVs, forty of which are seen here passing through Nelson Station behind Class 37 No. 37286. The locomotive trips from Radyr at 07.30 as the 9C82, and usually spends the day ferrying waste from colliery to tip, returning to Radyr in the early evening.

Plate 84 (right): An excellent picture of the 17.11 Cardiff (Central) to Rhymney train. It is formed of a three car Derby sub-▶urban unit and a three car Pressed Steel unit, and is seen curving north from Bargoed, on the last leg of its journey to the head of the valley.

Paul D. Shannon

Plate 82 (above): Class 37 locomotives, Nos. 37270 and 37231, arrive at Cwm Bargoed Station with a train of empty HAAs from Barry on 27th November 1982. In the background are the Taylor Woodrow sidings. The train is, however, bound for the sidings of A. J. Williams, as this company had a contract with the CEGB at the end of 1982.

Plate 83 (below): Another view of Cwm Bargoed, taken on 11th December 1982. Class 37 locomotives, Nos. 37254 and 37294, arrive with the 6093 service from Barry which will have to run down the line towards Dowlais to allow Nos. 37304 and 37275 to leave with the 6091 working to Aberthaw. With three trains in six hours on Saturdays, there is not much rest for the employees of A. J. Williams.

Plate 85 (above): The terminus at Rhymney used to have a flourishing coal depot, as well as Railfreight services conveyed on the 9C77, 23.10 service from Radyr. On 29th January 1983, the coal yard contained a solitary MCV, whilst a three car Derby suburban unit, No. C320, awaited departure with the 12.20 service to Barry Island. The coal depot is due for closure in May 1983, and the future of the branch from Bargoed has been questioned on several occasions.

Plate 86: Approaching Cwm Bargoed from the south, a pair of Class 37 locomotives are dwarfed by the steep sides of the Bargoed Taf Valley. During November 1982, of the six trains each week from A. J. Williams, three ran on Saturdays when this picture was taken.

Chapter Six

The rail network to the Merthyr and Treherbert valleys serves eight collieries, one coke works and the phurnacite works at Abercwmboi. In spite of the recent singling of the branch from Porth to Treherbert, an hourly passenger train runs eighteen hours each day, however, there are some two hour gaps in the timetable to Merthyr.

In many ways this area was the poor relation to the Rhymney Valley, with no merry-go-round services and all the freight traffic having to be remarshalled at Radyr. At the end of 1982, however, the colliery at Lady Windsor started dispatching coal in two merry-go-round services each day and at the time of writing, track renewal and modernization at Tower Colliery was underway to permit the heavier merry-go-round trains to load at this location.

Coal from Abercwmboi, Black Lion, Maerdy, Tymawr and Nantgarw is still marshalled at Radyr Yard, and any wagons needing repair at Powell Duffryn Wagon Works are also sent to Radyr. The yard dispatches trains to the main yards in South Wales and occasional 'block loads' of coal to Orgreaves. The coal depots at Cwmparc, Treforest, Rhymney and Merthyr are serviced from the yard although it is unlikely that this traffic will remain, as the Western Region intends to retain only two coal depots in South Wales, at Swansea and Newport. The prospect of more Railfreight in the area is good, as

Dowlow Steetley at Radyr have looked into the possibility of a conveyor link to the 'down' slow line at Taffs Well, this being able to handle above one million tons of stone each year. In addition to this, Penderyn Quarry may well have their contract with BR renewed, generating at least one extra train each day.

The phurnacite plant at Abercwmboi, opened in 1942 and extended on five occasions over the following thirty years, uses coal from eight different collieries and recycled 'breeze' from the three coke works in South Wales. Over one million tons of coal is carbonized annually, and most of this arrives by rail, with the phurnacite departing by rail at the end of the process. To cater for this traffic, there are two trains to Radyr and one to Penrhiwceiber, Merthyr Vale, Maerdy, Tower, Aberdare and Severn Tunnel Junction each day.

One of the smaller collieries in the area is Nantgarw, opened in 1922, and with a rail output of 1,200 tons each week. A small amount of this coal is shunted to the Nantgarw Coal Yard for retail sale, the rest being sent to the coke ovens at Nantgarw, Cwm and Coed Ely for further processing. Much of the shunting and trip working at Nantgarw is undertaken by a Class 08 shunter from Radyr, although most of the trains 'up the valleys' are, however, in the hands of the ubiquitous Class 37s.

Plate 87 (left): Abercynon is the point at which the Aberdare branch joins the Merthyr line and, as can be seen from this view, the track layout has been considerably rationalized since steam days. On 30th June 1982, Class 37 No. 37257 crosses on to the 'up' main line with the 8C70 Abercwmboi to Severn Tunnel Junction service, the train consisting of forty HTVs, four MCVs, one MDV and a guard's van (CAO). This load is much heavier than normal due to a derailment on the previous day causing the Aberdare branch to be blocked for 24 hours.

Plate 88 (above): On 3rd April 1979, Class 37 No. 37280 curves along the banks of the Taff, north of Radyr. Its train of coke from Abercwmboi includes a rake of old unfitted coke hoppers (HCO) at the end of the train.

Plate 89 (below): The 6079 Penallta Colliery to Aberthaw Power-Station working curves through Radyr Yard, on 2nd April 1981. Class 37 locomotives, Nos. 37292 and 37307, are running 3½ hours late with their load of coal, and have therefore been diverted down the 'big hill' from Aber to avoid the rush-hour at Cardiff (Central).

Plate 92 (right upper): A very rare visitor to Radyr is Class 37 No. 37024 from the Eastern Region. The engine is standing in Radyr Station with the 8C93 Black Lion Colliery to Ocean Washery service, which will run down through Cardiff (Central) and back up the Rhymney Valley line.

Plate 93 (right lower): At the south end of Radyr Yard is Radyr Quarry Junction. Here, during June 1982, Class 08 No. 08352 shunts wagons from the 'down' side to the 'up' yard. The shunter has a working code of 9E86 and, in this picture, is involved in the assembly of the 7C87 working to Llanelli.

Plate 90 (above): The 6C86 train arrives at Radyr Quarry Junction with cement from Aberthaw behind Class 47 No. 47230. The cement will travel west later in the evening on the 7C87 service to Llandeilo Junction, although its final destination is the Aberthaw cement terminal at Carmarthen.

Plate 91 (below): Gone are the days when, at tea-time, there were five trains queuing up to enter Radyr Yard. Of the forty or so timetabled departures from the yard each 24 hours, many are light engine movements, and an increasing number are cancelled due to lack of traffic. Much of this decrease can be put down to increasing merry-go-round facilities at collieries, removing the need for marshalling of coal at Radyr. Recent plans to rationalize the yard have suggested that no more than ten sidings are required for sorting if collieries such as Maerdy dispatch coal direct to Severn Tunnel Junction. On 13th July 1979, Class 37 No. 37286 leaves the yard with a northbound departure.

Plate 95 (above):   During the evening rush-hour, all merry-go-round services are routed via Radyr Quarry Junction to avoid Cardiff (Central). This practice will have to cease with the closure of Aber Junction to Walnut Tree Junction. Coming off the branch at Taffs Well are Class 37s, Nos. 37257 and 37295, with the 6091 Ocean to Aberthaw working.

Plate 96 (below):   Compounding the rail strikes of June 1982 was the fact that the miners joined the nurses and NHS ancillary workers in their strike, further reducing rail traffic in the South Wales valleys. Signalman Wayne Evans watches from the box as Class 37 No. 37178 passes with the 9C75, a special working of empties to Abercwmboi.

Plate 94 (left): Dominating this study of a three car Derby suburban diesel multiple unit is Castell Coch. Built in the 19th century and copying the style of the Rhine castles, it overlooks the Taff Gap which is the northern exit from Cardiff. On 25th September 1980, unit No. C313 scurries south to cater for the rush-hour traffic out of the capital.

Plate 97 (above): This rather unusual view was taken just south of Taffs Well during the winter of 1979. The street lamps from the nearby road provide excellent illumination for Class 37 No. 37243 and its train of 21½ ton hoppers bound for Abercwmboi.

Plate 98 (below): Towards the end of the working life of the 'Western' class locomotives, there were a large number of specials running as far afield as York and here, Class 52 No. D1010 *Western Campaigner* is deep in Western Region territory at Pontypridd. The 'Western Requiem' tour visited several of the valley lines on Saturday, 12th February 1977 and, indeed, the trip was so popular that it was repeated one week later.

Plate 99 (right): Stormsdown sidings, south of Abercynon, was once a busy marshalling yard for coal from Abercynon Pit and Lady Windsor Colliery. A three car Derby suburban unit, No. C317, approaches Abercynon with a Penarth to Merthyr train, as a Class 37 runs round its van in the distance. The Class 37 locomotive will pick up coal from Lady Windsor Colliery and take it down to Radyr.

Plate 100 (above): Empty ballast wagons for Penderyn Quarry have arrived at Aberdare on the 6C82 working from Radyr. Class 08 No. 08792 removes several 'cripples' under the watchful eye of the senior shunter at Aberdare.

Plate 102 (right upper): The points which guard the entrance to the Merthyr Coal Yard are padlocked and the sidings derelict. Just the hourly service to Cardiff remains and, on 29th January 1983, a three car Derby suburban diesel multiple unit, No. C300, is seen departing with the 11.00 service to Cardiff and Barry.

Plate 103 (right middle): The town of Trehafod provides the setting for this picture of a Barry to Treherbert train taken on 22nd June 1979.

Plate 104 (right lower): One wagon of the 9C91 Radyr to Aberdare working has been derailed at Abercynon, and this was not noticed until reaching Abercwmboi, by which time five miles of track had been damaged. Station staff at Aberdare supervise the shunting of the train by Class 37 No. 37306, as a sister locomotive, No. 37222, waits in the background with a southbound departure.

Plate 101 (below): The ballast for Penderyn is shunted into the BR exchange sidings at Hirwaun by Class 37 No. 37214, from where it will be picked up by the Rolls-Royce shunter from the quarry. One week after this picture was taken, on 13th December 1982, the train to the quarry ceased although, at the time of writing, it was thought that a new contract might re-establish the rail connection to the quarry.

Plate 105: Abercwmboi is unusual in that there are two trains timetabled to leave on Saturday mornings. Here, the first of these, the 6C70, 09.30 service to Radyr, accepts the single line token for the line to Abercynon. The train was made up of forty HTVs loaded with fuel nuts for Barry Docks and headed by Class 37 No. 37225. Coal bound for Ratho, Kittybrewster, Inverness and Galashiels, via Tweedmouth, was also present in the sidings on 26th March 1983.

Chapter Seven Cwm, Coed Ely and Tondu Branches

This short chapter deals with five freight only lines which sprout northwards from the South Wales main line between Llantrisant and Margam.

Cwm and Coed Ely lie at the end of two short branches which leave the main line at Llantrisant. Both have a colliery and a coke plant which are rail served, and each receives one visit from a Class 37 locomotive every morning. The Class 08 allocated to Llantrisant may, however, trip to the exchange sidings at Coed Ely (South) several times each day, bringing further loads of coal down to Mwyndy Yard.

Cwm Colliery was opened in 1912 and has a typical weekly output of 8,050 tons of coal. Some 2,800 tons of this goes to the Coed Ely Coking Plant, and a further 2,800 tons is transferred by an NCB locomotive to the coking plant at Cwm. Another 1,500 tons is sent direct to Margam Steelworks, 700 tons to British Benzole at Bedwas and the remaining 250 tons is sold as domestic coal. Cwm Coking Plant also receives coal from Tymawr and Nantgarw collieries.

The three branches which radiate from Tondu would appear, from the timetable, not to see much traffic. There are five trips in 24 hours to cover all three of them, with one additional trip to Mill Pit. However, once the trip engine has reached Tondu, it may travel up and down all three branches before returning to Margam, which means that the number of trains running north from Tondu is much greater than five. For example, on 22nd December 1981, the 9B88, 10.05 working from Margam started at Tondu and took empties up to Blaengarw, to return south with coal for Ogmore Vale Washery. It then took empties up to Wyndham and returned with 740 tons of coal for Ogmore Washery. Final departure for Margam was at 15.30, 6½ hours after starting, the trip being laden with coal bound for France via Newport Docks.

Two further branches in the area have been closed recently. One to Creigiau Quarry has now been dismantled, but the one to Wern Tarw has been kept intact in case British Rail win a contract with the local Rockwool Works. In closing this introduction, I should like to mention that the staff working on these five branches were the most friendly I have ever met anywhere on British Rail, and I thank them for the kind interest in my project.

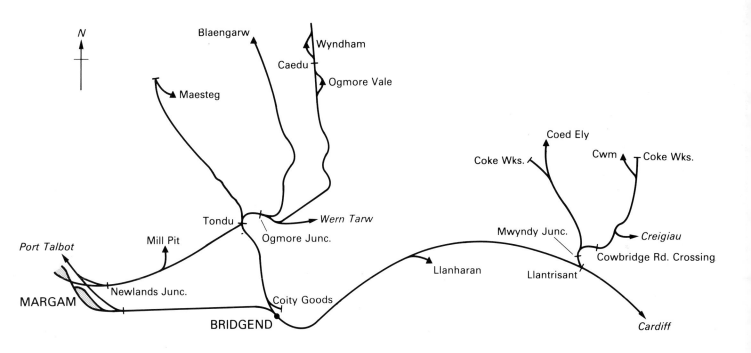

Plate 108 (above): Trip number three, and Driver Ranson collects the single line token from the signalman at Cowbridge Road Crossing box. Class 37 No. 37240 heads a rake of empty MDVs making up the 9096 trip working to Cwm Colliery.

Plate 109 (below): Having deposited the empty wagons in Cwm Colliery Class 37 No. 37240 prepares to depart with a train of coal for the Llanwern Steelworks.

Plate 106 (left upper): One morning in the summer of 1982, I actually managed to get up at 5a.m. At 6a.m. ex-BR Class 03 No. 2139 shunts loaded wagons before taking them to the lower yard at Coed Ely, from where they will be collected by the Llantrisant Class 08.

Plate 107 (left lower): Class 37 No. 37305 and Driver Ranson are already on their second trip of the morning when they arrive at Coed Ely Colliery at 8a.m. on 17th June 1982. On the left, ex-BR Class 03 No. 2139 is taking a rest from its early morning shunting duties.

Plate 110: On Thursday, 15th April 1982, Class 37 No. 37258 takes the first train of the week up the Maesteg branch, and is seen here approaching the site of the former station at Llangynwyd. The train is the 9B93 from Margam, and the five MDOs are conveying coal from Onllwyn, Coed Bach and Cynheidre to the National Fuel Distributors depot at Maesteg.

P. D. Shannon

Plate 111 (above): The miners at Blaengarw had been on strike for five days, on 22nd December 1981, because of a shortage of warm jackets for the work-force! For the first time in five days a train ascends the branch with empty wagons, this being the 9B88 Tondu to Blaengarw service which is leaving Tondu Station behind an unidentified Class 37.

Plate 112 (right): Maesteg has both a coal and distribution depot and a colliery. In the yard, on 15th April 1982, Class 37 No. 37258 shunts before proceeding as the 9B93 working with coal from the colliery to Ogmore Vale Washery via Tondu.

P. D. Shannon

Plate 113: On 21st December 1981, Class 37 No. 37306 passes Caedu signal box with coal from Wyndham Colliery to the washery at Ogmore Vale. After depositing its load in the washery, the Class 37 proceeded south to Margam with yet another trainload of coal.

Chapter Eight

MAIN LINE ~
Water Street Junction to Swansea (High Street)

The main line from Water Street Junction to Swansea passes through one of the most heavily industrialized areas in Britain and travelling towards Swansea, the first large installation is Margam Marshalling Yard. Completed in 1960 and designed to handle 5,000 wagons daily, it is a product of the 1950s modernization programme. The yard would have been of much more use if it had been built at Severn Tunnel Junction, but local industry persuaded BR that enough traffic would be generated to justify its construction. Subsequent contraction and closures have proved them seriously wrong.

There are forty departures each 24 hours to destinations within the Cardiff Division, and these account for most of the thousand wagons sorted each day at the yard. Shunting is conducted at the north end of the yard, although trains still arrive and depart past the closed hump at the south end of the complex. Other destinations to which trains travel are:

Banbury, Furzebrook, Stanlow and Whittington (all oil); Haverton Hill and Whitemoor (Speedlink); coil to Dee Marsh Junction, and lime empties to Tunstead. Other long distance freights travel to Crewe (Basford Hall), Ickles and Avonmouth. Margam Yard has assumed more importance since the closure of Llandeilo Junction Yard in October 1982, although it seems unlikely that the relatively small increase in traffic will justify reopening the hump.

As the train speeds northwards towards Port Talbot Station, the marshalling yard merges with the huge steelworks at Margam. This was opened in 1951 although a rail link to the construction site was established three years earlier in 1948. Iron-ore and coal arrive mainly by sea; the main rail input being lime, which arrives in air-braked covhops from Tunstead near Buxton. The rail output of the steelworks is, however, quite considerable. Hot rolled coil is despatched to Trostre, Velindre, Ebbw Vale and Shotton, this being sent out in block loads conveyed on 75.5 ton capacity BBAs.

The train slows to enter the station at Port Talbot and there are still steelworks on the left, although these are disused and are undergoing demolition. There have been steelworks on this site since before World War I, and it looks likely that they will remain for some time to come.

Next, Baglan Bay Chemical Works is on the left. Once a week it sends a train to Bridgwater and twice weekly to Hull (New) Yard, these complementing the twice daily departure to Barry. One mile further north is Court Salt Junction where nearly all freight trains leave the main line. In the remaining ten miles to Swansea, the main line crosses three freight only lines, and the complex geography of this area is best understood by careful study of the OPC Rail Atlas along with an Ordnance Survey map!

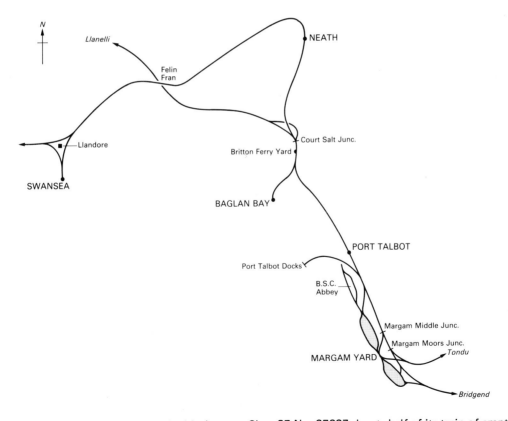

◄ *Plate 114 (left upper):* Blaengarw Colliery at its bleakest, as Class 37 No. 37227 shunts half of its train of empties under the loading gantry. In the background is coal for Ogmore Washery, which will travel south to Tondu where the engine will run round for the second half of the journey. The coal is bound for France via Newport Docks.

◄ *Plate 115 (left lower):* Later in the day, Class 37 No. 37227 waits at Wyndham Colliery for its load of 740 tons of coal for the washery at Ogmore. The engine has just run round its load of empties at Nant-y-Moel.

◄*Plate 116 (left upper):* Having run round its train at Margam Middle Junction, Class 37 No. 37288 climbs to cross over the South Wales main line at the start of its journey to Mill Pit. The train is the 9B88 to the Tondu valleys, and is made up of unfitted 21 ton mineral wagons (MDO).

◄*Plate 117 (left lower):* Leaving the other end of Margam Yard is Class 46 'Peak' No. 46004 with the 8C21, 08.10 Margam to Radyr service. The reception sidings of the disused hump can be seen in the background, half of which have already been removed. On 15th June 1982 six had been retained, in case of an upturn of traffic which would justify reopening the hump.

Plate 118 (above): Many groups hire trains to London, particularly during June and July for school trips. One such train is seen here, passing Margam at Water Street Junction, behind Class 47 No. 47147.

Plate 119 (below): On 11th August 1978, Class 37 No. 37304 runs round at Margam Moors Junction, having arrived from Tondu. The OBAs have come from the paper mill at Tondu and the coal is from Maesteg Colliery. The train will cross the main line to run into the reception sidings from the west.

Plate 120 (above): An unidentified Class 37 leaves Margam with a trip to Tondu. In the background there are two Class 47 locomotives with the 4C31 arrival from Velindre *(left)*, and the 6C22, 07.00 Severn Tunnel Junction to Llandeilo Junction *(right)*. Class 08 No. 08361 shunts in the wagon repair sidings.

Plate 121 (left): Taken in 1978, this shot gives an impression of the size of Margam Yard. Although designed to handle 5,000 wagons each day, it was only dealing with 1,000 at this time, and the hump was closed shortly after this picture was taken.

Plate 122 (below): Four years later, in 1982, and there are far fewer wagons in the yard than in 1978 *(above)*. Class 37 locomotives, Nos. 37180 and 37265, await departure with the 6C30 10.30 Margam to Severn Tunnel Junction working, which runs via the Vale of Glamorgan. The train carries steel billets from Abbey Works on air-braked bogie bolsters (BBAs).

Plate 123: One of South Wales's now famous iron-ore trains accelerates away from the signal at Margam after a crew change. On 15th June 1982, this train, the 6C32, 08.15 from Llanwern, was hauled by Class 56 locomotives Nos. 56043 and 56041. During the later part of 1982 these trains only ran for two or three days each week, due to the decreased demand for iron-ore at Llanwern.

Plate 124: Class 37 No. 37235 passes Abbey Steelworks with a train of ballast comprising grampus and sea lion hoppers. I was forcibly removed from this bridge by an over enthusiastic BSC policeman, who threatened to confiscate my camera. Over my dead body!

Plate 125: The three blast furnaces in the background are out of use and awaiting demolition. Class 37 No. 37279 heads the 6B86 Swansea (Burrows) to Severn Tunnel Junction train past the old Port Talbot Steelworks, with coal for various depots around the country.

Plate 126:   Deep in the steelworks complex, Class 56 locomotives, Nos. 56040 and 56046 descend the dock branch with the 6C53, 14.35 Llanwern to Port Talbot Docks service on 30th March 1983. The engines park their train at the entrance to the loading gantry, and pick up a pre-loaded train of iron-ore for Llanwern.

Plate 127: On the left is the iron-ore terminal at Port Talbot. On the right, the 'second man' checks with the terminal as to which line to enter with his train of empties from Llanwern. The train is hauled by Class 56 locomotives, Nos. 56046 and 56040.

Plate 128: Approaching Port Talbot Station from the east is the 7C01 MWFO Margam to Velindre working. Class 37 No. 37300 has had to depart two hours early in order to be off the Swansea avoiding line by the afternoon, when it will be occupied by engineers working in Lonlas Tunnel.

Plate 131 (right upper): With a load of mainly scrap metal, Class 47 No. 47068 passes Briton Ferry with the 7C43, 10.25 Severn Tunnel Junction to Llandeilo Junction working on 15th June 1982. Baglan Bay Chemical Works form the background, and in the centre of the picture the Briton Ferry Yard pilot can just be seen.

Plate 132 (right lower): The line on the left is the 'down' Swansea avoiding line, the 'up' line passing under the main line at this point and joining it ¼ mile further east. Class 33 No. 33057 canters east with a short parcels train made up of four NKVs.

Plate 129 (above): Workmen replace some sleepers on the 'up' slow line at Port Talbot Station, oblivious to Class 47 No. 47061 passing with the 6V64 MSX Albion Gulf to Herbrandston service. This particular train was sent west via the Llandore loop, due to trouble in Lonlas Tunnel.

Plate 130 (below): Having just joined the main line at Court Sart Junction, Class 37 locomotives Nos. 37185 and 37204 accelerate east with the 6091 Blaenant to Aberthaw merry-go-round working of 18th June 1982.

Plate 133: Photographed on 17th October 1970, the empty working of the 'South Wales Pullman' pauses at Llandore on its way to Swansea (High Street) Station. Resignalling and the introduction of HSTs make this photograph a piece of history.

Wyn Hobson

Plate 134: Standing alone at the buffers at Swansea (High Street) Station is a three car Swindon cross-country unit, No. C615. It will depart at 14.05 with a through service to Pembroke Dock, taking one minute over two hours for the 73 mile journey.

Of the two branches running north-east from Neath & Brecon Junction, the busier is the Onllwyn line, there being three collieries up this line, the first of which is Blaenant. With five merry-go-round departures each day, it is by far the largest contributor to the needs of Aberthaw Power-Station. Most of the trains run from Blaenant to Aberthaw, reversing at Jersey Marine South Junction, but five each week depart as separate workings from Jersey Marine Steel Supply sidings. As well as five merry-go-round diagrams each day, there are five trips from either Swansea (Burrows) or the docks to Onllwyn. The sidings at Onllwyn are stocked from Banwen Colliery and Onllwyn Pit. They send their coal in old unfitted MDOs on the 22 mile journey to Swansea Docks.

The line to Aberpergwm is a remnant of the old Great Western Vale of Neath Line. Several collieries along this valley have closed in recent years, leaving just Aberpergwm with its daily train to Swansea Docks. As for traffic in the western direction from Burrows sidings, there is the daily 9F23 trip to Morriston and the visits of the yard pilot to Port Tennant Wagon Workshops.

The most interesting place to visit in this area is Swansea Docks. Miles of half buried track, old bullhead rail, vintage coal 'drops' and extravagant signalling make this a fascinating place to spend Saturday afternoon!

The most important part of the introduction to this chapter is the map which, hopefully, helps to untangle the maze of lines on the eastern side of Swansea.

Swansea Docks is, without doubt, the largest exporter of coal in South Wales. Trains run to Swansea (Burrows) and Swansea Docks from a wide area, including the collieries at Cynheidre, Onllwyn and Aberpergwm. There are also many trains from other yards in South Wales and they are as follows:

East Usk (2), Margam (3), Pantyffynnon (4), Pembrey (2), Radyr and Severn Tunnel Junction (2). Most of this coal is for export, but some may be remarshalled at Swansea (Burrows) sidings for redistribution in South Wales, while the large domestic coal depot at Swansea (East) also claims a portion of the coal brought into the dock area. This coal depot is one of only two in South Wales which are expected to last into 1984 and, as such, is going to be modernized to accept Speed-link coal hoppers (HEA).

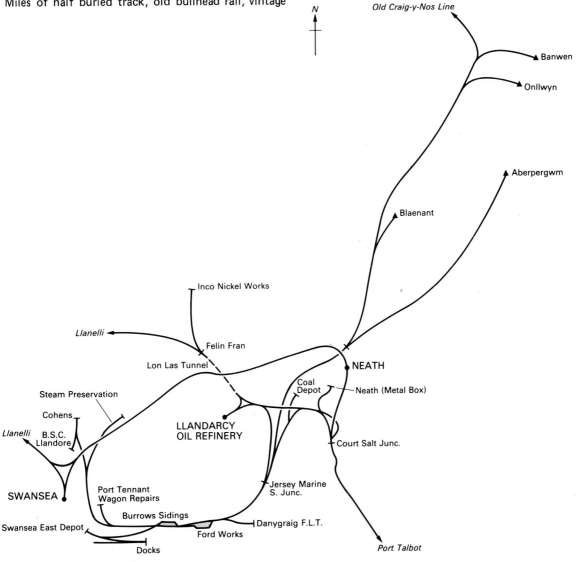

Plate 135: As far as the railway is concerned, time has stood still for over fifty years in Swansea Docks. The complex junctions, bullhead rail and extravagant signalling are all remnants of a prosperous but less efficient age. Class 37 No. 37162 leaves Swansea Docks with a rake of unfitted mineral wagons (MDO and MCO) making up the 9B80 freight working to Pantyffynnon.

Plate 136: In June 1974, Class 08 No. 08656 approaches Swansea (Burrows) sidings with the local trip from Morriston and Port Tennant Wagon Repair Works. *Wyn Hobson*

Plate 137: This impressive industrial landscape was photographed in February 1972, and shows the trip working from Bird's Yard at Morriston to Swansea (Burrows) pausing at the site of Upper Park Station. The line leading to the right is the extended siding to the Imperial Smelting Works at Llansamlet (demolished soon after this picture was taken). The Llansamlet and Morriston lines are all that remain of the Midland Railway, Swansea (St. Thomas) to Brynamman section. The line crossing the lower Swansea Valley in the middle distance is the main line to Paddington. *Wyn Hobson*

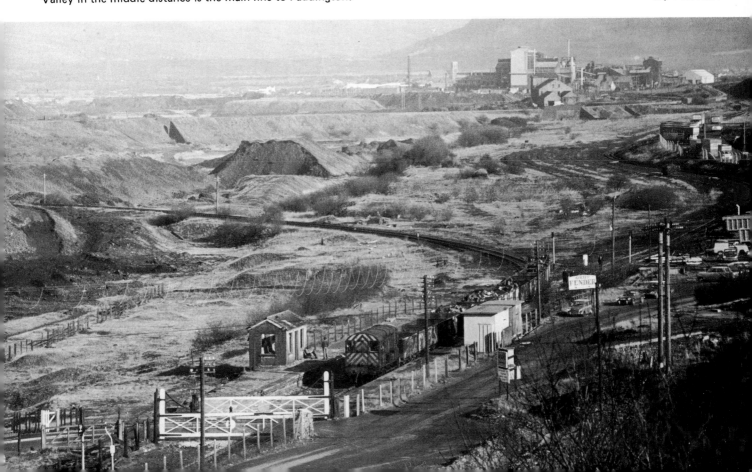

Plate 138: On the afternoon of 15th June 1982, Class 08 No. 08663 shunts in Swansea (Burrows) sidings.

Plate 139: All that remains of the old Vale of Neath Line is the branch to Aberpergwm Colliery, the other collieries served by this line having lost their rail links in recent years. On a gloomy morning, in June 1982, Class 37 No. 37293 waits at the colliery whilst the crew have their morning cup of tea. The locomotive will eventually leave at the head of the 9B84 train to Swansea Docks, conveying anthracite fuel nuts to the docks in unfitted wagons (MDO).

Plate 140: The sidings at Onllwyn are served by five workings each day from Swansea Docks or Burrows sidings. Here the 9B77 afternoon working from the colliery passes the site of Seven Sisters Station behind Class 37 No. 37232.

Plate 141: Coal from Banwen and Onllwyn is picked up by British Rail from the sidings at Onllwyn. This view shows Class 37 No. 37232 about to leave with the 9B77 service to Swansea, while the train visible in the background is the 9F23 arrival from Swansea Docks, hauled by Class 37 No. 37301.

Plate 142: On 16th April 1982, Class 37 No. 37236 passes through Blaenant Colliery with the 9B77 from Onllwyn to Swansea (Eastern) Depot, formed of a mixture of 21 ton hoppers (HTV) and 21 ton mineral wagons (MDO).

P. D. Shannon

Plate 143: After running round its train of 38 empty MDOs, an unidentified Class 37 begins to reverse into the sidings at Onllwyn. The working is the 9B77 from Swansea Docks, and the date is 16th April 1982. In the top right-hand corner of the picture the trackbed of the former branch to Craig-y-Nos can be seen, this having only recently been lifted.

P. D. Shannon

Many a railway enthusiast must have visited Llandore Shed and wondered why there were no freight workings travelling to West Wales passing along the Llandore Loop. This is, in fact, only used as a diversionary route when the Swansea avoiding line is blocked for one reason or another.

There are usually over twenty 'up' and twenty 'down' trains along the Swansea avoiding line each day. Most of these run during the night, and many may be retimed to fit in with extensive engineering work being undertaken in Lonlas Tunnel. Starting at the east end of the line, the first junction after Llandarcy is Felin Fran. Here the branch to the Inco Nickel Works at Clydach on Tawe turns north and on the opposite side of the line is a small coal depot, which is amongst those listed for closure by the end of this year. Next, at Llangyfelach Junction, is the entrance to the Velindre Tinplate Works. Although smaller than the works at Trostre, there are three timetabled departures to Margam each day but, in practice, only one or two run on any given day.

Five miles further west is Grovesend Colliery loop, which is the entrance to Brynlliw Colliery which, until 1982, supplied 6,000 tons of coal to Aberthaw Power-Station each week. The trains would load standing on the main line at Pontardulais coal stocking site, blocking the 'up' line for two hours. Perhaps because of this and new merry-go-round services from the Cardiff valleys, these trains no longer run.

At Morlais, the Swansea avoiding line meets the Central Wales line, and rail traffic can turn either south to Llanelli or north to Llandovery. Although there is no through freight traffic on the Central Wales line, there is a considerable volume of coal transported on the southern section of this line. Pantyffynnon is the centre for this traffic, most of which runs south on six daily trains to Swansea Docks, with an additional fitted coal train at 00.50 to Severn Tunnel Junction. The two Class 08 locomotives allocated to Pantyffynnon are busy all day shunting between Wernos Washery, Betws Drift and Pantyffynnon Yard. There are three daily trips up the Aman Valley, one to Gwaun-cae-Gurwen and two to Abernant.

The only freight train regularly seen north of Pantyffynnon is the 9B96 MWFO, 07.05 Llanelli to Landovery. The 61½ mile round trip is undertaken by a single Class 03 taking coal to the distribution depots at Llanedeilo and Llandovery. This trip is unlikely to continue if the coal depots along the line are closed, but it will remain the author's favourite train even if somewhat out of place in a modern 125m.p.h. British Railways environment.

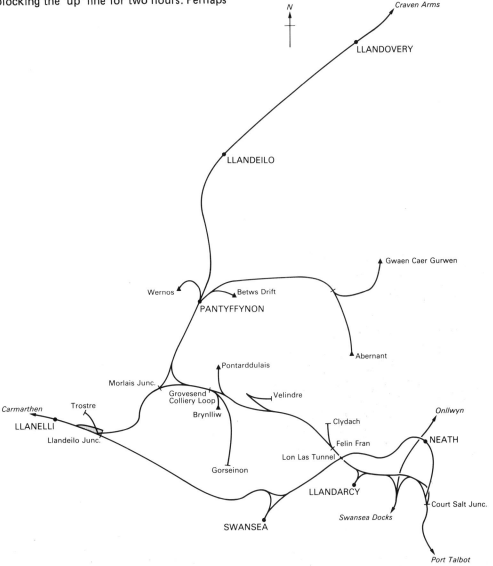

Plate 144: Deep in the Welsh countryside, north of Llandeilo at Rhosmaen, Class 03 No. 03141 hauls the MWFO Llandovery to Llandeilo Junction Yard trip. When the 'Mainline' model of a Class 03 came on to the market, this train was ideal for the smallest model railway layout.

Plate 145: The 9B96 train shunts at Llandovery on 18th June 1982. Explosives in two VWVs were collected by the army from the goods depot within five minutes of the train's arrival, while the other three wagons (MDV and MCV) contained coal from Deep Navigation Colliery for the coal merchant at Llandovery. Class 03 No. 03141 only spent fifteen minutes shunting the train before it returned south at its maximum speed of 25m.p.h.

Plate 146: Whilst waiting for the 10.08 Swansea to Shrewsbury train, passengers shelter from the rain at Llandeilo Junction. The two car Metro-Cammell unit (Nos. W51515 and W51445) rolls into the station past the three times weekly Llandovery to Llanelli freight working.

Plate 147: Pantyffynnon is at the junction of the Abernant branch and the Central Wales line. Metro-Cammell diesel multiple units Nos. 51517, 51446, 50933 and 51566 are seen entering the station with the 12.25 Swansea to Shrewsbury service.

Plate 148 (left upper):   On 28th January 1983, the 10.08 Swansea to Shrewsbury train is seen at Pantyffynnon, formed of Swindon three car cross-country unit No. C616, and two car Metro-Cammell Nos. M51177 and M56351. The prominent stop sign is for the benefit of trips shunting from Wernos to Pantyffynnon sidings.

Plate 149 (left lower):   Hidden deep in the washery at Wernos is Class 08 No. 08660, on loan to the NCB. The NCB commonly borrows shunting locomotives from BR, and Wernos is one of the regular places at which they are deployed.

Plate 150 (above): Coal from Bettws Drift is washed at Wernos. Here a load of cleaned coal leaves the washery and joins the Central Wales line, to the North of Pantyffynnon Station, behind Class 08 No. 08660. The coal will reach its destination, Swansea Docks, on the 9B96, 14.00 Pantyffynnon to Swansea (Burrows).

Plate 151 (below):   Empties from Wernos Washery, eventually bound for Gwaun-cae-Gurwen, pass through Pantyffynnon Station behind Class 08 No. 08354. The two Class 37 locomotives, which will take the empties up the valley to Gwaun-cae-Gurwen, can be seen in the distance on the right.

Plate 152: Ammanford Station, long closed to passengers, still sees regular coal trains from Gwaun-cae-Gurwen, Abernant and Bettws Drift. Here Class 37 locomotives, Nos. 37251 and 37239, wait for the gates to be opened before easing their way down into Pantyffynnon Yard.

Plate 153: Two Class 37s stand in the sidings at Pantyffynnon with the lunch-time arrival from Gwaun-cae-Gurwen, while Class 08 No. 08769 busies itself putting a van on the back of the 9F36, 13.55 departure for Abernant.

Plate 154: Crawling up the incline at Cwmrose Branch Junction, Class 37 No. 37239 heads a rake of thirty loaded MDOs containing coal from Bettws Drift for the washery at Abernant. Another Class 37 brings up the rear of the train.

Plate 155: Class 37 locomotives, Nos. 37284 and 37286, shunt in the exchange sidings at Gwaun-cae-Gurwen. In the background is the ex-BR Class 08 used by the NCB to transfer wagons from the colliery to the exchange sidings. The loaded mineral wagons on the left contain coal for export via Swansea Docks.

Plate 156: Abernant Colliery is at the end of the branch line from Pantyffynnon and is served by two trains each day, most of the coal being bound for Swansea Docks. Class 08 No. 08637 makes its rather drunk way along almost buried trackwork at the colliery during June 1982.

Plate 157: Empty BBAs and a CAO make up the 8C48 Llandeilo Junction to Margam working. The train is seen here, on 17th June 1982, at Grovesend Colliery loop, running two hours early and headed by Class 37 No. 37176.

Plate 158: In April 1978 both Brynlliw and Graig Merthyr collieries employed steam engines to do their shunting. Glimpsed whilst rushing from Graig Merthyr to Brynlliw is Class 47 No. 47236, accelerating east with a Brynlliw to Aberthaw merry-go-round service.

Plate 159: Although Felin Fran signal box is boarded up, it is still used as a ground frame to allow access to the Clydach branch. On the left a solitary MCV, in Felin Fran Coal Depot, frames Class 37 No. 37293 as it drifts west 'engine and van'. After the Class 37 had cleared the section, the civil engineering department took possession of the line to work in Lonlas Tunnel.

Plate 160: Having come under the M4 at Brynlliw, Class 46 No. 46004 heads west with the 7C43, 10.25 Severn Tunnel Junction to Llandeilo Junction working. The train is made up of one MCV containing coal, one RBV pallet van and seven MCVs containing scrap.

Chapter Eleven

Llanelli, Cynheidre and Cwmmawr

I have devoted a separate chapter to Llanelli and its branches because, until recently, it was the terminus for most wagon-load freight from the west. Since the closure of Llandeilo Junction Yard, it has been largely bypassed. The yard had 22 local departures every 24 hours, and services to Haverton Hill and March Whitemoor Yard. Since the yard's closure, Margam Yard has accommodated eight extra departures and ten extra arrivals, with up to ten further trains being routed to Swansea Docks, Margam or Carmarthen Bay Power-Station at Pembrey. One departure that still runs from Llanelli is the MWFO to Llandovery, hauled by a Class 03 throughout.

Llanelli is served by hourly trains to Swansea and Milford Haven, with additional through trains on weekdays to Shrewsbury, and one each to Cardiff and London. Recent improvements have brought Southern Region Class 33 locomotives to West Wales, and these now haul all but one of the Milford trains. The Shrewsbury service remains in the hands of the trusty Swindon three car cross-country diesel multiple units, with occasional help given by Metro-Cammell units from the Midland Region. During 1980, the Carmarthen to Paddington train became the first regular working of an HST west of Swansea.

The branch lines to Cynheidre Colliery and Cwmmawr Colliery are included in this chapter. Five trains each day wind their way down the tortuous branch from Cynheidre, these being previously marshalled at Llandeilo Junction Yard but now running directly to the power-station at Burry Port or to the docks in Swansea. If coal is needed elsewhere in South Wales, then trainloads are run to Margam where they are re-sorted.

The line to Cwmmawr Colliery, often referred to as the Burry Port & Gwendraeth Valley Line (BPGV), is traversed three times daily by the 9F25 trip. The limited clearance at several points along the line means that specially adapted Class 03 locomotives with cut down cabs are the only engines permitted to operate on this stretch. To bring 600 tons of coal from Cwmmawr requires three engines, making the line rather un-usual with daily triple-headed trains. This practice will cease when the new connection from Coed Bach, to south of Kidwelly, is built .

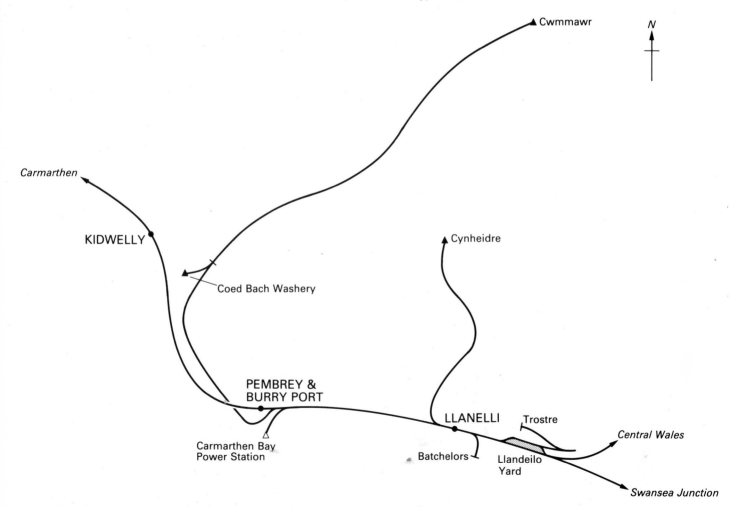

Plate 161 (right upper): This Class 37, No. 37232, has been languishing in Llanelli Goods Shed for two days and now, on 17th ▶ June 1982, it is being run 'light engine' to Llandore for repairs.

Plate 162 (right lower): Another view of the Llanelli stabling point, taken later the same day, shows Class 47 locomotives, Nos. ▶ 47150 and 47408, resting between turns. Class 08 No. 08400 has just come up from Batchelor Robinson and is crossing the main line to enter the stabling point.

Plate 163: A busy scene glimpsed at the old Llandeilo Junction Yard with, from left to right, Class 46 No. 46004 with the 6C59, 13.50 to Severn Tunnel Junction service, then Class 37 No. 37235 with the 9B83 arrival from Cynheidre and Class 33 No. 33026 passing at the head of the 13.05 Swansea to Milford Haven working.

Plate 164: In a cloud of fumes, Class 37 No. 37278 accelerates through the western outskirts of Llanelli with its train of empties forming the 9B75, 13.05 Swansea (Burrows) sidings to Burry Port and Pembrey. The wagons will eventually be refilled at Cwm-mawr Colliery at the head of the Burry Port & Gwendraeth Valley Line.

Plate 165: Cynheidre Colliery lies five miles north of Llanelli at the end of a steep and winding branch. Shunting loaded MDOs at the colliery, on 17th June 1982, is Class 37 No. 37235. Eventually the train will depart as the 9B83 service to Llandeilo Junction, the coal being bound for Swansea Docks.

Plate 166: Deep in the woods north of Llanelli is the 13.27 Llandeilo Junction Yard to Cynheidre working, running over an hour late. Because of the thick foliage, it was not possible to see the number of this particular Class 37.

Plate 170 (above): This, the only picture of a Class 35 'Hymek' in the book, was taken on 21st March 1969, when the author was only eight years old! Class 35 No. D7094 heads empty coaching stock west through Llanelli Station.

Wyn Hobson

Plate 171 (below): The partially dismantled Duports Steelworks forms the background in this view of Class 33 No. 33008. The locomotive heads a GUV and four Mk. I coaches on the 14.40 Fishguard to Swansea (High Street) working.

Plate 167 (left upper): On 30th March 1983 the 6C52, 10.55 Fishguard to Margam Speedlink service is relegated to a Class 7 freight, by the unfitted mineral wagons at the rear of the train, on which Class 37 No. 37285 passes Llandeilo Junction exactly on time. The sorry sight of disused sidings can be seen on both sides of the line.

Plate 168 (left middle): HST Unit No. 253022 whistles past Llandeilo Junction Yard with the 16.40 Paddington to Carmarthen train. On the left, Class 37 No. 37124 waits for the 20.15 to Whitemoor to be marshalled correctly before departing on its long journey to the Fens.

Plate 169 (left lower): An evening visit to Llandeilo Junction Yard with a friend was rewarded by the appearance of Class 56 No. 56038 *Western Mail* with the 4C44, 18.20 Margam to Trostre coil train. The headlights of the locomotive stand out, as the train is photographed at dusk while shunting in Trostre Tinplate Works.

Plates 172 & 173:   These two views show *(top)* Class 03 locomotives, Nos. 03152, 03119 and 03144, shunting at Coed Bach Washery after depositing a train of coal for washing. Then *(below)*, two pulling and one pushing, the trio ascend the Burry Port & Gwendraeth Valley Line with empty mineral wagons for Cwmmawr Colliery.

Chapter Twelve

The first eleven chapters of this book have dealt with the industrial part of South Wales. In this, the final chapter, we cover the rural south-west of Wales. It is 73½ miles by rail from Swansea to Fishguard or, in other words, further away than the Severn Tunnel. However, traffic is much lighter along this stretch of line.

There are twenty departures heading west from Swansea (High Street) each day, eight of these running through to Milford Haven and four to Fishguard Harbour. Five of the trains run as far as Llanelli, where they reverse at the start of their 110 mile journey along the Central Wales line to Shrewsbury. Of the remaining four, two run to Pembroke Dock and two terminate at Carmarthen. The passenger service was greatly improved by the introduction to the area, in May 1982, of Class 33 locomotives and these now cover the majority of passenger diagrams to Milford Haven. The Pembroke Dock branch, which is divided into two sections of 15¾ miles and 11½ miles by the crossing point at Tenby, has seven 'up' and seven 'down' trains each weekday.

The freight traffic west of Burry Port is divided into block oil trains to the refineries at Milford Haven, and wagonload traffic to all other locations.

The recent introduction of air-braked rolling stock to the far west was heralded as an extension of the Speedlink network. The new trains thus described are the 6C52 Fishguard to Margam and the 6C62 Milford to Margam services, although most reports fail to mention that these 'improvements' include the total closure of Llandeilo Junction Yard. Initially, the traffic on these new trains will be oil and government stores (explosives etc.) while the remaining mixed freight traffic, which is mainly coal for household use, is catered for by the 7C14, 03.40 departure from Margam. This train is unusual in that it runs to Milford on Mondays and Thursdays, Fishguard on Tuesdays and Fridays and Carmarthen on Wednesdays.

Oil traffic from the refineries at Herbrandston, Robeston and Waterston has decreased considerably over the last five years. The only trains to run every day are the 6A18, 05.20 Robeston to Theale Murco and the 6M50, 15.45 Waterston to Albion Gulf. Trains also run to Hereford, Holywell Junction, Kingsbury, Langley, Micheldever, Oakleigh, Newton Abbot, Thatcham and Uskmouth, although most of these locations only receive one train each week.

Perhaps one of the highlights of a journey west from Swansea is not a large motive power depot or busy marshalling yard, but two beautiful stretches of line. The first is along the Afon Tywi, between Kidwelly and Carmarthen, and the second is through Letterston Gorge, on the descent to Fishguard. Hopefully, the pictures in this chapter will encourage you to make the journey!

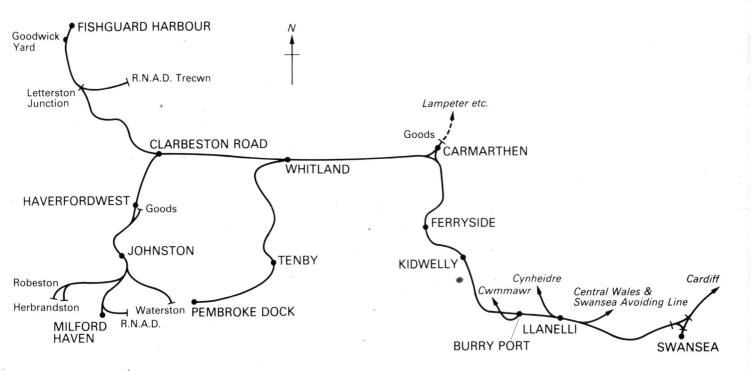

Plate 174: The estuary of the River Loughour is crossed by the westbound railway at two points, these being at Morfa Mawr, by the Swansea avoiding line, and here at Loughour, by the main line from Swansea to Fishguard. This photograph was taken from the site of Roman ruins which, much to the annoyance of the archaeologists, extend under the main line. The train is the 07.30 Milford Haven to Swansea service, hauled by Class 33 No. 33033, one of the few services to have 'on train' sorting of mail.

Plate 175: The mail coaches pictured above return west on the 17.15 Swansea to Milford Haven working. Class 47 No. 47105 brakes to enter Burry Port Station, in Great Western semaphore signalling territory for the first time since leaving Swansea.

Plate 176: One of the most beautiful stretches of railway in the country is the line along the coast from Kidwelly to Carmarthen. Winding its way along the best-known section, at Ferryside, is the 16.10 service from Swansea to Pembroke Dock and Milford Haven. The train, which is made up of a three car Metro-Cammell diesel multiple unit and a three car Swindon cross-country diesel multiple unit, will split at Whitland, this being the junction for the Pembroke Dock branch.

Plate 177: One mile south of Ferryside the line curves sharply through ninety degrees and, at this point, there is more than a passing resemblance to the Dawlish sea wall in Devon. Some 237 miles from London (via Gloucester), the 08.30 Milford Haven to Swansea working canters along behind Class 33 No. 33021 on 2nd October 1982.

Plate 178: Class 33 No. 33001 brings the 09.37 Milford Haven to Swansea service into Carmarthen Station, where the train will reverse. Carmarthen was once served by two stations, Junction Station and the Town Station, which was the gateway to the Westwalean hinterland. Services to Aberystwyth, via Lampeter and the rather unusually named Strata Florida, ceased in 1964, and the line was finally closed to all traffic at the end of 1973. A short section of the line from Bronwydd Arms to Penybont has been preserved by the Gwilli Railway.

Plate 179: The goods yard at Carmarthen used to cater for coal to Newcastle Emlyn and milk from Pont Llanio and Green Grove, as well as local traffic. Since the withdrawal of freight services to the north, in 1973, the goods yard has been poorly used and, as can be seen from this photograph, has fallen into disrepair. On 2nd September 1982, Class 37 No. 37266 stands on the bridge over the Avon Tywi, whilst waiting to pick up any traffic from the yard for the 7C48 Haverfordwest to Margam working.

Plate 180: Coming to the end of the 27 mile long Pembroke Dock branch, a three car Swindon cross-country unit, No. C616, winds its way on to the main line at Whitland. The branch is served by seven 'up' and seven 'down' trains each weekday, and the one pictured is the 10.15 Pembroke Dock to Swansea service.

Plate 181: The end of the line at Pembroke Dock. Swindon cross-country unit No. C621 waits to depart with the 13.15 working to Whitland, where passengers change for Swansea. The small terminus at Pembroke Dock is served by a through train to Paddington on summer Saturdays which, with the Saturdays only Tenby to York working, is the only time locomotives are brought on to the branch.

Plate 182: During August 1982, Naval equipment leaves RNAD Milford behind Class 47 No. 47129, at the start of its long journey to Rosyth in Scotland. The first leg of the journey is made as the 7C45 Milford Haven to Haverfordwest service, after which Margam, Severn Tunnel Junction, Warrington (Arpley), Carlisle (Kingmoor), Newton-on-Ayr, Mossend and Dunfermline will be calling points. The reason for the large number of 'ports of call' is that the train is vacuum-fitted, made up of vans (VMW and VEV) and open wagons (SOV), and these cannot be incorporated into the air-braked Speedlink network.

Plate 185 (right upper): Four coaches is a rather light load for Class 47 No. 47125 with the 07.44 Cardiff to Milford Haven service, seen here entering Haverfordwest. The station at Haverfordwest caters for the inhabitants of the town, whilst the goods yard handles local traffic and 'service facilities' for the oil refineries, which includes wagon repairs and fuel.

Plate 186 (right lower): Later, on the same day in August 1982, Class 33 No. 33024 awaits departure with the 13.05 Swansea to Milford Haven working. The driver looks expectantly along the platform as the station staff finish unloading the mail.

Plate 183 (above): With the exception of the 11.00 Swansea to Milford train, pictured here at Johnston, all of the Swansea to Milford Haven workings have been locomotive-hauled since May 1982. Unlike most junctions on British Rail which are contracting, Johnston has actually expanded since the construction of rail links to the refineries at Robeston, Herbrandston and Waterston. In this view, on 27th August 1982, a Swindon three car cross-country unit, No. C615, is seen rushing through Johnston non-stop.

Plate 184 (below): Waterston Oil Refinery used to dispatch six trains each day to the Midlands and the West Country. The extensive track layout is now somewhat under-used as, on 27th August 1982, the refinery had only two trains due out, one to Albion and the other to Heathfield. This depression was caused by a decrease in demand, more oil being moved by pipeline, and the fact that output is always lower in the summer. Class 47 No. 47342 waits while its train, the 6M50 to Gulf Albion, is loaded as it passes under the large gantry on the right. Also of interest is that the refinery provides employment for ex-BR Class 03 shunters, Nos. 2046 and 03113.

Plate 187:   A major railway junction in the middle of nowhere is Clarbeston Road, where the 11.05 Swansea to Milford Haven train slows before leaving the main line on 2nd October 1982. The post in front of the signal box is used by trains from Fishguard to return the single line token, thus avoiding the necessity to stop. However, this outdated operating practice will soon disappear along with the Great Western lower quadrant signals, when the area is put under the control of a new panel box at Clarbeston. The tell-tale signs of concrete troughing and a new signal post suggest that it will only be a matter of weeks before the change takes place.

Plate 188:   A terrain more in keeping with the West Highland main line provides the backdrop for Class 33 No. 33009 as it speeds west past Wolf's Castle with the 12.00 service from Swansea to Fishguard Harbour. To 'stop' the train as it passed, a shutter speed of one thousandth of a second was necessary.

Plate 189: The daily freight working to Fishguard leaves Llandeilo Junction at the unearthly hour of 04.25. Having arrived at the western extremity of the Cardiff Division, it trips to Trecwn with stores of supplies for the Royal Naval Armaments Depot. The dew still glistens on the rails as Class 37 No. 37266 prepares to leave the sidings at Trecwn with nine vans (VVV) forming the 7C15 service to Fishguard. The crew who signed on at 04.00 will be back in Llanelli by 13.00 in time for lunch.

Plate 190: The end of the line, and yet another Class 33 stands with the 14.40 working to Swansea. Although Fishguard is a similar size to Haverfordwest, it has only three departures each day; two of these are boat-trains to London and the other to Swansea. A connecting bus service operates to Haverfordwest for those unlucky enough to miss their train.

Plate 191: And so I finish this book with the panorama of Letterston Gorge. The 13.15 Fishguard to Paddington boat-train winds its way through the beautiful Westwalean countryside behind Class 47 No. 47033, at the start of its 260 mile journey to the capital.